Accelerated Christian Training Series

Laying the FOUNDATION

BOOK 2

THE NATURE OF MAN

Dr. Mark Hanby

© Copyright 2001 — Mark Hanby Ministries

All rights reserved. This book is protected by the copyright laws of the United States of America. This book may not be copied or reprinted for commercial gain or profit. The use of short quotations or occasional page copying for personal or group study is permitted and encouraged. Permission will be granted upon request. Unless otherwise identified, Scripture quotations are from the New King James Version of the Bible. Scripture quotations marked KJV or AMP are taken from the King James Version and the Amplified Bible, respectively. Emphasis within Scripture quotations is the author's own. Please note that Destiny Image's publishing style capitalizes certain pronouns in Scripture that refer to the Father, Son, and Holy Spirit, and may differ from some Bible publishers' styles.

Take note that the name satan and related names are not capitalized. We choose not to acknowledge him, even to the point of violating grammatical rules.

Destiny Image® Publishers, Inc.
P.O. Box 310
Shippensburg, PA 17257-0310

"Speaking to the Purposes of God for This
Generation and for the Generations to Come"

ISBN 0-7684-2143-8

For Worldwide Distribution
Printed in the U.S.A.

This book and all other Destiny Image, Revival Press,
MercyPlace, Fresh Bread, Destiny Image Fiction,
and Treasure House books are available
at Christian bookstores and distributors worldwide.

For a U.S. bookstore nearest you, call **1-800-722-6774**.
For more information on foreign distributors,
call **717-532-3040**.
Or reach us on the Internet: **www.destinyimage.com**

Contents

	Introduction	5
I.	**The Nature of Man**	9
	A. Who Were Adam and Eve?	
	B. For What Purpose Did God Create Adam and Eve?	
	C. Why Did God Create Both a Man and a Woman?	
	D. What Agreement Did God Make With Man?	
II.	**The Fall of Man**	29
	A. How Did Sin Enter the World?	
	B. What Was Man's True Sin at the Fall?	
	C. What Was the Result of Man's Rebellion Against God?	
	D. What Was the Result of Sin Entering Into the World?	
	E. What of the Nature of God Is Revealed in His Response to Fallen Man?	
	F. Why Did God Send Man out of the Garden?	
	G. How Is It That All Men Are Born Under the Curse of Sin That Adam Committed?	
III.	**The Seed of Rebellion Continues**	51
	A. What Was Man's Attitude After He Sinned in the Garden?	
	B. What Were the Effects of Rebellion After the Garden?	
	C. How Would God's Purpose in Man Continue?	
	D. What Did God Command Noah to Do?	
	E. How Did Noah Acknowledge God's Authority Over His Life After He Came Out of the Ark?	
	F. What Was Man's Response to This New Beginning Following the Obedience of Noah?	
	G. How Did Man, With His Knowledge of Good and Evil, Begin to Build a New World?	
	H. Why and How Did God Stop the Building of the City and the Tower?	
	I. What Is the Spiritual Meaning of Babylon to Us?	

Introduction

And you shall know the truth, and the truth shall make you free (John 8:32).

What Is Truth?

Truth Is a Person

"What is truth?" Pilate asked Jesus (Jn. 18:38). The answer to Pilate's timeless question was standing before him. Truth is not a series of facts or the sum of information. Truth is a Person: Jesus Christ. Jesus said of Himself, "I am the way, the truth, and the life" (Jn. 14:6). Truth is not only rational, it is relational. Religious theory that only teaches about God can never liberate the soul. True freedom is found in knowing Him. "And ye shall know the truth, and the truth shall make you free" (Jn. 8:32).

God has chosen to unfold His relational truth in various ways throughout the Bible and always in the form of personal relationship between Himself and men such as Adam, Noah, and Abraham. The unfolding revelation of God's relationship with man was spelled out in agreements between God and man called covenants. What better way to unfold a relational truth than in the context of relationship?

Truth Is the Result of Seeking Jesus

This relational truth is more than experience. Despite his great experience on the road to Damascus, the apostle Paul did not end his search for truth but wrote, "...that I may know *Him* and the power of His resurrection, and the fellowship of His sufferings..." (Phil. 3:10, emphasis mine). Job, wounded and in distress, cried out, "Oh that I knew where I might find *Him*..."

The Nature of Man

(Job 23:3). Jesus said, "Blessed are those who hunger and thirst for righteousness, for they shall be filled" (Mt. 5:6). Our finding the truth is the result of a hunger to know the Person of Jesus Christ. We do not seek truth and find Jesus; we seek Jesus and find the truth.

Truth Is a Highway

We may think of truth as a highway—an endless journey into the Person of God. All of us walking in the light of relationship with God are at some point in that journey. As we "seek the Lord" and "search the Scriptures," we advance. The **A**ccelerated **C**hristian **T**raining **S**eries has been created to help us move on in that journey into the Lord regardless of whether we are new believers or seasoned saints of God. There is always more truth for us regardless of our place along the road. "His ways [are] past finding out" (Rom. 11:33b).

It is important that every believer follow a course such as this. Although the believer may be exposed to a variety of good biblical preaching, there must be a systematic seeking after truth to provide a foundation upon which to grow in relationship with the Person of Jesus. Imagine agreeing to marry someone of whom you had only seen a pencil sketching. It is our intention in this course of seeking to paint a full and vital portrait of the Christ who is alive in you.

If you are a new traveler on the highway of truth, you have begun the most exciting journey of your life. Many parallels can be drawn between the new believer and a newborn child. It would be a criminal act to leave an infant out in the cold or in a house without someone to give him attention and care. It is likewise a tragedy when the Church does not nurture newborn Christians. If newborns are going to be healthy and grow to

Introduction

maturity, they must be carefully and loving fed with the truth of the Word.

Truth Brings Maturity

The Christian life is a "growing up into Him in all things...until we come to the measure of the stature of the fullness of Christ" (see Eph. 4:13-15). It is important that we place ourselves under pastoral care if we are to "grow up." Even Jesus, who astonished the doctors and lawyers of His time, was entrusted to His parents' care. The Bible says, "Obey thse who rule over you, and be submissive: for they watch out for your souls" (Heb. 13:17). To reject the care of pastoral oversight is to reject God's plan to bring us to Himself and to leave ourselves open to error and the exit from the highway of our journey into the truth.

The ministry that God has given to the Church is five-phased with a threefold purpose. Ephesians 4:11 tells us that God has placed in the church apostles, prophets, evangelists, pastors and teachers. Their purpose is to mature, feed and motivate believers in their own calling and ministry. Only when this equipping is established in the life of the believer will they progress from spiritual newborn to spiritual childhood and on to spiritual adulthood.

In the life of every Christian there must come a point where we "put away childish things" (1 Cor. 13:11). As we become "rooted and grounded" in the basic principles of faith we are "no more children, tossed to and fro, and carried about with every wind of doctrine" (Eph. 4:14). As we grow and mature in the faith we are able to rise above our own problems and trials and reach out with power and confidence to minister the truth to the needs of those around us.

How the Accelerated Christian Training Series Works

The **A**ccelerated **C**hristian **T**raining **S**eries has been designed to meet the crucial need for intensive training in the basic doctrines of the Christian faith. These doctrines are revealed in the context of relationship between God and man. It is designed as a self-instruction course in which believers can journey at their own pace. You will find review questions at the end of each section of material you have studied that will help you to retain what you've learned.

There is an exercise called "Dig a Little Deeper; Grow a Little Closer" at the end of each major section. These reflective questions are designed to help you synthesize the truths you have been taught and then apply them in a personal way. You will be invited to journal throughout the study of this book to provide you with a record of your new understanding and growth in God. Journaling will help you to grow in your ability to hear God's voice and adjust your life and understanding to His purpose.

Following this **A.C.T.S.** course will stimulate and accelerate your spiritual understanding and bring you to a more intimate knowledge of the Truth, who is Jesus Christ. We pray that you will grow in the awareness of the Lord's presence as He guides you to Himself through the study of His Word.

Two Companions for the Road

During this time of new growth in your spiritual life there will be questions that come to mind. You will meet two companions throughout this series on the road to truth. They are Newly Newborn and Truly Taughtright. Newly will ask some of the same questions that you ask, and Truly, his mentor, will give the answers.

I. The Nature of Man

A. Who Were Adam and Eve?

1. Adam and Eve were the first man and woman created by God and placed on the earth.

Then God said, "Let Us make man in Our image, according to Our likeness; let them have dominion over the fish of the sea, over the birds of the air, and over the cattle, over all the earth and over every creeping thing that creeps on the earth." So God created man in His own image; in the image of God He created him; male and female He created them (Genesis 1:26-27).

2. Just as God Himself is one God with three parts, God created Adam as a three-part being: flesh by which he relates to the world, soul by which he relates to himself, and spirit by which he can relate to God.

Now may the God of peace Himself sanctify you completely; and may your whole spirit, soul, and body be preserved blameless at the coming of our Lord Jesus Christ (1 Thessalonians 5:23).

For the word of God is living and powerful, and sharper than any two-edged sword, piercing even to the division of soul and spirit, and of joints and marrow, and is a discerner of the thoughts and intents of the heart (Hebrews 4:12).

The Nature of Man

B.   For What Purpose Did God Create Adam and Eve?

1.   Adam and Eve were created to glorify God and give Him pleasure.

And the glory which You gave Me I have given them, that they may be one just as We are one...Father, I desire that they also whom You gave Me may be with Me where I am, that they may behold My glory which You have given Me; for You loved Me before the foundation of the world (John 17:22,24).

For of Him and through Him and to Him are all things, to whom be glory forever. Amen (Romans 11:36).

Therefore, whether you eat or drink, or whatever you do, do all to the glory of God (1 Corinthians 10:31).

The Nature of Man

You are worthy, O Lord, to receive glory and honor and power; for You created all things, and by Your will they exist and were created (Revelation 4:11).

2. Adam and Eve were created to have an intimate relationship with God.

And they heard the sound of the Lord God walking in the garden in the cool of the day (Genesis 3:8a).

I will dwell among the children of Israel and will be their God (Exodus 29:45).

And He said, "My Presence will go with you, and I will give you rest" (Exodus 33:14).

That which we have seen and heard we declare to you, that you also may have fellowship with us; and truly our fellowship is with the Father and with His Son Jesus Christ (1 John 1:3).

3. Adam and Eve were created to have dominion over all other creatures.

Then God said, "Let Us make man in Our image, according to Our likeness; let them have dominion over the fish of the sea, over the birds of the air, and over the cattle, over all the earth and over every creeping thing that creeps on the earth" (Genesis 1:26).

You have made him to have dominion over the works of Your hands; You have put all things under his feet (Psalm 8:6).

4. Adam and Eve were created to care for the garden in which God had placed them.

Then the Lord God took the man and put him in the garden of Eden to tend and keep it (Genesis 2:15).

C. **Why Did God Create Both a Man and a Woman?**

1. God created both Adam and Eve because Adam could not fulfill God's purpose by himself. Eve was created as a "help meet."

And the Lord God said, "It is not good that man should be alone; I will make him a helper comparable to him" (Genesis 2:18).

And the Lord God caused a deep sleep to fall on Adam, and he slept; and He took one of his ribs, and closed up the flesh in its place. Then the rib which the Lord God had taken from man He made into a woman, and He brought her to the man. And Adam said: "This is now bone of my bones and flesh of my flesh; she shall be called Woman, because she was taken out of Man" (Genesis 2:21-23).

2. God created both Adam and Eve so that they could set an example for all future husbands and wives in their love for each other.

And Adam said: "This is now bone of my bones and flesh of my flesh; she shall be called Woman, because she was taken out of Man." Therefore a man shall leave his father and mother and be joined to his wife, and they shall become one flesh (Genesis 2:23-24).

The Nature of Man

So husbands ought also to love their own wives as their own bodies; he who loves his wife loves himself. For no one ever hated his own flesh, but nourishes and cherishes it, just as the Lord does the church. For we are members of His body... (Ephesians 5:28-30).

3. God created Adam and Eve and gave them the power of creation to populate the earth.

Then God blessed them, and God said to them, "Be fruitful and multiply; fill the earth and subdue it" (Genesis 1:28a).

D. What Agreement Did God Make With Man?

1. God said He would provide man with all that he needed for life. Man was to depend totally upon God's power and wisdom for his life.

And the Lord God commanded the man, saying, "Of every tree of the garden you may freely eat" (Genesis 2:16).

The Nature of Man

But seek first the kingdom of God and His righteousness, and all these things shall be added to you. Therefore do not worry about tomorrow, for tomorrow will worry about its own things. Sufficient for the day is its own trouble (Matthew 6:33-34).

2. Man was not to eat from the tree of the knowledge of good and evil and thus be independent from God. If he did he would be separated from God and would die spiritually.

But of the tree of the knowledge of good and evil you shall not eat, for in the day that you eat of it you shall surely die (Genesis 2:17).

Let's Review What We Have Learned About the Nature of Man.

1. _____ and _____ were the first man and woman created by God and placed on the earth.

2. *Then God said, "Let Us make man in Our _____, according to Our likeness; let them have _____ over the fish of the sea, over the birds of the air, and over the cattle, over all the earth and over every creeping thing that creeps on the earth"* (Genesis 1:26).

3. List two of the reasons why God created man.

_____

_____

4. Man was not to eat from the tree of the _____ of good and evil and thus be _____ from God.

The Nature of Man

5. God created Adam as _____ part being. Can you name the parts? _____

6. God would provide man with _____ that he needed for life. Man was to _____ totally upon God's power and wisdom for his life.

Dig a Little Deeper; Grow a Little Closer

1. Read Matthew 6:25-34.

2. God supplies us with all that we will ever need just like He told Adam that He would. What then should we seek instead of worrying about what we need? List areas of concern that you have for the things that you need and then submit them to the Lord.

_____
_____
_____
_____
_____
_____
_____

The Nature of Man

Review Notes

The Nature of Man

The Nature of Man

The Nature of Man

The Nature of Man

The Nature of Man

The Nature of Man

The Nature of Man

The Nature of Man

The Nature of Man

The Nature of Man

The Nature of Man

The Nature of Man

II. The Fall of Man

A. How Did Sin Enter the World?

1. Sin entered into the world through Adam's choice to rebel against God's agreement and be independent from God.

So when the woman saw that the tree was good for food, that it was pleasant to the eyes, and a tree desirable to make one wise, she took of its fruit and ate. She also gave to her husband with her, and he ate (Genesis 3:6).

Therefore, just as through one man sin entered the world, and death through sin, and thus death spread to all men, because all sinned—(For until the law sin was in the world, but sin is not imputed when there is no law. Nevertheless death reigned from Adam to Moses, even over those who had not sinned according to the likeness of the transgression of Adam, who is a type of Him who was to come...) (Romans 5:12-14).

For as by one man's disobedience many were made sinners, so also by one Man's obedience many will be made righteous (Romans 5:19).

2. Sin entered the world when satan, in the form of a serpent, created doubt in Eve's mind about what God said.

Now the serpent was more cunning than any beast of the field which the Lord God had made. And he said to the woman, "Has God indeed said, 'You shall not eat of every tree of the garden'?" And the

The Nature of Man

woman said to the serpent, "We may eat the fruit of the trees of the garden" (Genesis 3:1-2).

3. Sin entered the world as satan created doubt as to the provision of God.

"But of the fruit of the tree which is in the midst of the garden, God has said, 'You shall not eat it, nor shall you touch it, lest you die.'" Then the serpent said to the woman, "You will not surely die" (Genesis 3:3-4).

4. Sin entered into the world as satan created doubt as to man's relationship and dependence upon God.

For God knows that in the day you eat of it your eyes will be opened, and you will be like God, knowing good and evil (Genesis 3:5).

5. Sin still enters through these same areas of temptation: the lust of the flesh, the lust of the eyes, and the pride of life.

So when the woman saw that the tree was good for food [the lust of the flesh], *that it was pleasant to the eyes* [the lust of the eyes], *and a tree desirable to make one wise* [the pride of life], *she took of its fruit and ate. She also gave to her husband with her, and he ate* (Genesis 3:6).

Do not love the world or the things in the world. If anyone loves the world, the love of the Father is not in him. For all that is in the world—the lust of the flesh, the lust of the eyes, and the pride of life—is not of the Father but is of the world. And the world

The Fall of Man

is passing away, and the lust of it; but he who does the will of God abides forever (1 John 2:15-17).

B. **What Was Man's True Sin at the Fall?**

   1. Man's true sin was disobedience in acting on his own, independent of God, which is an act of rebellion.

   2. Man's true sin was taking his life into his own hands.

C. **What Was the Result of Man's Rebellion Against God?**

   1. As a result of rebellion their eyes were opened and they knew they were naked.

Then the eyes of both of them were opened, and they knew that they were naked (Genesis 3:7a).

   2. As a result of rebellion shame entered into the world.

They knew that they were naked (Genesis 3:7a).

The Nature of Man

3. As a result of rebellion they sewed fig leaves to provide a covering for their shame.

And they sewed fig leaves together and made themselves coverings (Genesis 3:7).

4. As a result of rebellion they tried to hide from the presence of God among the trees of the garden. Fear had entered into the world.

And they heard the sound of the Lord God walking in the garden in the cool of the day, and Adam and his wife hid themselves from the presence of the Lord God among the trees of the garden (Genesis 3:8).

So he said, "I heard Your voice in the garden, and I was afraid because I was naked; and I hid myself" (Genesis 3:10).

As it is written: "There is none righteous, no, not one...There is no fear of God before their eyes." Now we know that whatever the law says, it says to those who are under the law, that every mouth may be stopped, and all the world may become guilty before God (Romans 3:10;18-19).

D. What Was the Result of Sin Entering Into the World?

The result of the entrance of sin into the world was separation from God and spiritual death.

Eternal life to those who by patient continuance in doing good seek for glory, honor, and immortality;

but to those who are self-seeking and do not obey the truth, but obey unrighteousness—indignation and wrath (Romans 2:7-8).

Therefore, just as through one man sin entered the world, and death through sin, and thus death spread to all men, because all sinned (Romans 5:12).

For the wages of sin is death, but the gift of God is eternal life in Christ Jesus our Lord (Romans 6:23).

Then, when desire has conceived, it gives birth to sin; and sin, when it is full-grown, brings forth death (James 1:15).

E. **What of the Nature of God Is Revealed in His Response to Fallen Man?**

    1.   The justice of God is revealed in the pronunciation of three curses upon those in the garden.

So the Lord God said to the serpent, "Because you have done this, you are cursed more than all cattle, and more than every beast of the field; on your belly you shall go, and you shall eat dust all the days of your life. And I will put enmity between you and the woman, and between your Seed and her seed; He shall bruise your head, and you shall bruise His heel" (Genesis 3:14-15).

To the woman He said, "I will greatly multiply your sorrow and your conception; in pain you shall bring forth children; your desire shall be for your

The Nature of Man

husband, and he shall rule over you" (Genesis 3:16).

Then to Adam He said, "Because you have heeded the voice of your wife, and have eaten from the tree of which I commanded you, saying, 'You shall not eat of it'; cursed is the ground for your sake; in toil you shall eat of it all the days of your life" (Genesis 3:17).

2. The mercy of God was revealed in that while God knew that Adam sinned He still came looking for him.

Then the Lord God called to Adam, and said to him, "Where are you?" (Genesis 3:9)

3. The grace of God is revealed in His provision for covering the shame of Adam and Eve's sin.

Also for Adam and his wife the Lord God made tunics of skin, and clothed them (Genesis 3:21).

The Fall of Man

F. Why Did God Send Man out of the Garden?

God sent man out of the garden so that he could not eat of the tree of life and live forever in his fallen condition, forever separated from God.

Then the Lord God said, "Behold, the man has become like one of Us, to know good and evil. And now, lest he put out his hand and take also of the tree of life, and eat, and live forever"—therefore the Lord God sent him out of the garden of Eden to till the ground from which he was taken (Genesis 3:22-23).

G. How Is It That All Men Are Born Under the Curse of Sin That Adam Committed?

All men are descended from Adam who chose to rebel against God and forfeit the blessings of intimate relationship with God for which he was created.

And He has made from one blood every nation of men to dwell on all the face of the earth, and has determined their preappointed times and the boundaries of their dwellings (Acts 17:26).

For as in Adam all die, even so in Christ all shall be made alive (1 Corinthians 15:22).

For all have sinned and fall short of the glory of God (Romans 3:23).

The Nature of Man

Let's Review What We Have Learned About the Fall of Man.

1. Sin came into the world through Adam's _____ to go against God's agreement and be _____ from God.

2. *For as by one man's _____ many were made sinners, so also by one Man's obedience many will be made righteous* (Romans 5:19).

3. Sin entered the world as satan created _____ as to the provision of God.

4. The result of the entrance of sin into the world was _____ from God and spiritual death.

5. What were three things were revealed about the nature of God in His response to man's fall into sin?

_____

_____

_____

The Fall of man

6. What animal form did satan use to create doubt in Eve's mind about God? _____

Dig a Little Deeper; Grow a Little Closer

1. Remember the three things that satan tries to use to tempt us: the lust of the flesh, the lust of the eyes, and the pride of life? In another account, the temptation of Jesus Christ in the wilderness, satan used these same ploys. Read about them in Matthew 4:1-11.

2. Compare what Jesus was tempted with and how He responded each time. For example, how did Jesus respond to satan when satan told Jesus to turn stones into bread?

_____

_____

_____

_____

_____

3. Are there places in your life where you struggle against temptation? Where have you not yet fully trusted God for His provision? Pray into those areas, submitting them in total dependence upon the Lord.

_____

_____

_____

_____

The Nature of Man

Review Notes

The Fall of Man

The Nature of Man

The Fall of Man

The Nature of Man

The Fall of Man

The Nature of Man

The Fall of Man

The Nature of Man

The Fall of Man

The Nature of Man

The Fall of Man

The Nature of Man

III. The Seed of Rebellion Continues

A. **What Was Man's Attitude After He Sinned in the Garden?**

    1. Man's attitude was one of rebellion. He wanted to be free from God.

    2. Man believed that he had a better way to meet his needs than God did.

    3. Man believed the words of the serpent, that he could be like God.

B. **What Were the Effects of Rebellion After the Garden?**

    1. Adam and Eve's first cooperative effort—the birth of Cain—produced the fruit of man's rebellion. The seed of rebellion that was planted in Adam led to murder in only one generation when Cain killed his brother Abel.

The Nature of Man

Now Adam knew Eve his wife, and she conceived and bore Cain, and said, "I have acquired a man from the Lord." Then she bore again, this time his brother Abel. Now Abel was a keeper of sheep, but Cain was a tiller of the ground...Now Cain talked with Abel his brother; and it came to pass, when they were in the field, that Cain rose up against Abel his brother and killed him (Genesis 4:1-2,8).

2. Rebellion and evil increased among men to the extent that God could no longer tolerate it.

Then the Lord saw that the wickedness of man was great in the earth, and that every intent of the thoughts of his heart was only evil continually. And the Lord was sorry that He had made man on the earth, and He was grieved in His heart (Genesis 6:5-6).

3. God had no choice but to destroy the man whom He created. He would destroy man by a great flood.

So the Lord said, "I will destroy man whom I have created from the face of the earth, both man and beast, creeping thing and birds of the air, for I am sorry that I have made them" (Genesis 6:7).

And behold, I Myself am bringing floodwaters on the earth, to destroy from under heaven all flesh in which is the breath of life; everything that is on the earth shall die (Genesis 6:17).

C. **How Would God's Purpose in Man Continue?**

1. Everyone on the earth was not to be destroyed. A man called Noah, righteous in

The Seed of Rebellion Continues

his generation, found grace in the eyes of God.

But Noah found grace in the eyes of the Lord. This is the genealogy of Noah. Noah was a just man, perfect in his generations. Noah walked with God (Genesis 6:8-9).

2. In Noah, man would get a second chance. In Noah we learn the principle that God always preserves a remnant through which His purpose is performed.

Then the Lord said to Noah, "Come into the ark, you and all your household, because I have seen that you are righteous before Me in this generation" (Genesis 7:1).

And now for a little while grace has been shown from the Lord our God, to leave us a remnant to escape, and to give us a peg in His holy place, that our God may enlighten our eyes and give us a measure of revival in our bondage (Ezra 9:8).

The remnant will return, the remnant of Jacob, to the Mighty God (Isaiah 10:21).

Isaiah also cries out concerning Israel: "Though the number of the children of Israel be as the sand of the sea, the remnant will be saved" (Romans 9:27).

D.   What Did God Command Noah to Do?

1. God gave Noah instructions to build an ark—a large boat—to save himself, his family, and the animal life God had created.

The Nature of Man

Make yourself an ark of gopherwood; make rooms in the ark, and cover it inside and outside with pitch. And this is how you shall make it: The length of the ark shall be three hundred cubits, its width fifty cubits, and its height thirty cubits. You shall make a window for the ark, and you shall finish it to a cubit from above; and set the door of the ark in its side. You shall make it with lower, second, and third decks (Genesis 6:14-16).

2. Noah obeyed God in every detail.

Thus Noah did; according to all that God commanded him, so he did (Genesis 6:22).

By faith Noah, being divinely warned of things not yet seen, moved with godly fear, prepared an ark for the saving of his household, by which he condemned the world and became heir of the righteousness which is according to faith (Hebrews 11:7).

The Seed of Rebellion Continues

E. How Did Noah Acknowledge God's Authority Over His Life After He Came Out of the Ark?

1. Noah built an altar upon which to offer a sacrifice to the Lord.

Then Noah built an altar to the Lord, and took of every clean animal and of every clean bird, and offered burnt offerings on the altar (Genesis 8:20).

2. As a result of Noah's acknowledgment of God's authority God renewed His promise to man.

And the Lord smelled a soothing aroma. Then the Lord said in His heart, "I will never again curse the ground for man's sake, although the imagination of man's heart is evil from his youth; nor will I again destroy every living thing as I have done" (Genesis 8:21).

3. As a result of Noah's acknowledgment God renewed His purpose in man to fill the earth.

So God blessed Noah and his sons, and said to them: "Be fruitful and multiply, and fill the earth" (Genesis 9:1).

4. God gave the sign of the rainbow to confirm the promises He made to Noah.

"I set My rainbow in the cloud, and it shall be for the sign of the covenant between Me and the earth"...And God said to Noah, "This is the sign of the covenant which I have established between Me

The Nature of Man

and all flesh that is on the earth" (Genesis 9:13,17).

F. **What Was Man's Response to This New Beginning Following the Obedience of Noah?**

  1. Man responded with more rebellion. The sinful nature that resulted from the rebellion of Adam was still in man.

  Then the Lord saw that the wickedness of man was great in the earth, and that every intent of the thoughts of his heart was only evil continually (Genesis 6:5).

  2. Man continued to rebel against authority as Ham, the son of Noah, shamelessly looked upon his father, who was uncovered, and made him an object of ridicule before the other sons.

The Seed of Rebellion Continues

And Noah began to be a farmer, and he planted a vineyard. Then he drank of the wine and was drunk, and became uncovered in his tent. And Ham, the father of Canaan, saw the nakedness of his father, and told his two brothers outside (Genesis 9:20-22).

G. **How Did Man, With His Knowledge of Good and Evil, Begin to Build a New World?**

    1.   Man continued his rebellion. Nimrod, a mighty hunter and a descendant of Noah's son Ham, began to build the Babylonian civilization.

Cush begot Nimrod; he began to be a mighty one on the earth. He was a mighty hunter before the Lord; therefore it is said, "Like Nimrod the mighty hunter before the Lord." And the beginning of his kingdom was Babel, Erech, Accad, and Calneh, in the land of Shinar (Genesis 10:8-10).

    2.   Man began to build human civilization without God's wisdom and authority. He built a great city and a great tower to accomplish his own purpose.

Now the whole earth had one language and one speech. And it came to pass, as they journeyed from the east, that they found a plain in the land of Shinar, and they dwelt there. Then they said to one another, "Come, let us make bricks and bake them thoroughly." They had brick for stone, and they had asphalt for mortar (Genesis 11:1-3).

The Nature of Man

3. Man built the great tower out of his desire to be independent from God. He wanted to build a great empire that would glorify man rather than God.

And they said, "Come, let us build ourselves a city, and a tower whose top is in the heavens; let us make a name for ourselves, lest we be scattered abroad over the face of the whole earth" (Genesis 11:4).

4. Man attempted to reach into heaven just as satan had tried to ascend to the throne of God in his own rebellion. Man deliberately opposed the charge of God to fill the earth by consolidating in one place.

Then God blessed them, and God said to them, "Be fruitful and multiply; fill the earth and subdue it" (Genesis 1:28a).

So God blessed Noah and his sons, and said to them: "Be fruitful and multiply, and fill the earth" (Genesis 9:1).

H.   Why and How Did God Stop the Building of the City and the Tower?

1. God stopped the building because His wrath was against man's rebellion. God hates the independent nature of man that thinks he can make it on his own.

But the Lord came down to see the city and the tower which the sons of men had built (Genesis 11:5).

The Seed of Rebellion Continues

2. God stopped the building because man's rebellion could spread like an infection to all men. Man with the knowledge he had would continue to build and grow farther away from God.

And the Lord said, "Indeed the people are one and they all have one language, and this is what they begin to do; now nothing that they propose to do will be withheld from them" (Genesis 11:6).

3. God stopped man's rebellious building by confusing their language and scattering them throughout the earth. This ended the concentration of rebellion and evil.

"Come, let Us go down and there confuse their language, that they may not understand one another's speech." So the Lord scattered them abroad from there over the face of all the earth, and they ceased building the city (Genesis 11:7-8).

4. God stopped the building of Babel, which means "the gate of god." Their city and its tower was their way to God. Babel in God's language means "confusion" or "mingle."

Therefore its name is called Babel, because there the Lord confused the language of all the earth; and from there the Lord scattered them abroad over the face of all the earth (Genesis 11:9).

The Nature of Man

I. **What Is the Spiritual Meaning of Babylon to Us?**

1. The tower was built to glorify human wisdom and independence from God. The substitution of human government and wisdom in place of God's revelation through His Word will always fail.

Do not be wise in your own eyes; fear the Lord and depart from evil (Proverbs 3:7).

Woe to those who are wise in their own eyes, and prudent in their own sight! (Isaiah 5:21)

Be of the same mind toward one another. Do not set your mind on high things, but associate with the humble. Do not be wise in your own opinion (Romans 12:16).

2. We must seek to totally restore biblical Christianity—the one true faith.

The Seed of Rebellion Continues

Beloved, while I was very diligent to write to you concerning our common salvation, I found it necessary to write to you exhorting you to contend earnestly for the faith which was once for all delivered to the saints. For certain men have crept in unnoticed, who long ago were marked out for this condemnation, ungodly men, who turn the grace of our God into lewdness and deny the only Lord God and our Lord Jesus Christ (Jude 1:3-4).

3. We must be separated from man-made religion (Babylonian systems). We are to look to the Bible for direction and not human wisdom. We must allow the Holy Spirit to lead us into God's way and away from man's way.

Let's Review What We Have Learned About the Seed of Rebellion

1. Man's attitude was one of _____. He wanted to be _____ from God.

2. _____ and evil increased among men to the extent that God could no longer _____ it.

3. God destroyed the earth by a great _____.

4. A man called _____, righteous in his generation found _____ in the eyes of God.

5. God always preserves a _____ through which His purpose is performed.

The Nature of Man

6. Man began to build human civilization without God's _____ and _____.

7. God stopped man's rebellious building by confusing their _____ and _____ them throughout the earth.

8. The substitution of _____ government and _____ in place of God's revelation through His Word will always _____.

Dig a Little Deeper; Grow a Little Closer

1. Considering the account of the tower of Babel, man was acting in a way that was totally opposite from the commission of God to Adam and later to Noah and his sons. What was the commission that God gave to both Adam and again to Noah? See the verses below and the many times that God gave this same commission.

> *Then God blessed them, and God said to them, "Be fruitful and multiply; fill the earth and subdue it"* (Genesis 1:28a).

> *So God blessed Noah and his sons, and said to them: "Be fruitful and multiply, and fill the earth"* (Genesis 9:1).

> *Also God said to him: "I am God Almighty. Be fruitful and multiply; a nation and a company of nations shall proceed from you, and kings shall come from your body"* (Genesis 35:11).

2. Our fruitfulness in God's purposes depends upon our view of God. What was it that God told Jacob about Himself in Genesis 35:11 that would enable Jacob to be fruitful?

The Seed of Rebellion Continues

_____

_____

3. In what area(s) of your life would you desire to bear more fruit? Family? Finances? Witness? Others? Your growth in those areas of life will depend upon your view of God. Is God the Almighty One in that area where you desire growth? Pray about those areas, acknowledging God as the sole authority and source of growth. List the areas you pray for and write out a prayer turning them over to the Lord.

_____

_____

_____

_____

The Nature of Man

Review Notes

The Seed of Rebellion Continues

The Nature of Man

The Seed of Rebellion Continues

The Nature of Man

The Seed of Rebellion Continues

The Nature of Man

The Seed of Rebellion Continues

The Nature of Man

The Seed of Rebellion Continues

The Nature of Man

The Seed of Rebellion Continues

The Nature of Man

The Seed of Rebellion Continues

Be sure to enter into the journal in this book how God responds to what you have prayed.

Books in the *Laying the FOUNDATION* Series:

Book 1—The Nature of God
- I. The Nature of God
- II. The Bible
- III. The Creation

Book 2—The Nature of Man
- I. The Nature of Man
- II. The Fall of Man
- III. The Seed of Rebellion Continues

Book 3—A Call to Faith and Obedience
- I. Abraham: The Father of Faith and Obedience
- II. Israel: Called to Be the People of God

Book 4—From Covenant to Kingdom
- I. Taking Possession of the Promises of God
- II. Establishing the Kingdom
- III. The Message of the Prophets
- IV. Restoring the Remnant of Israel

Book 5—The New Covenant
- I. The New Covenant
- II. The Person of Jesus Christ
- III. The Nature of Jesus Christ
- IV. The Humiliation of Jesus Christ

Book 6—Jesus Christ, Servant of God
- I. Wounded for Our Transgressions
- II. Bruised for Our Iniquities
- III. Chastised for Our Peace
- IV. Scourged for Our Healing

Book 7—The Exaltation of Christ
- I. The Exaltation of Jesus Christ
- II. Jesus and the Kingdom of God

Summary

More Titles by Dr. Mark Hanby

➤ YOU HAVE NOT MANY FATHERS

"My son, give me your heart." So says the proverb, echoing the heart and passion of our Father in heaven. God has spiritual "dads" all over the world whom He has filled with wisdom, knowledge, compassion, and most of all, love for those young in the faith. You do not have to go through your life untrained and unloved; uncared for and forgotten. There are fathers in Christ who are waiting to pour all they have into your heart, as Elijah did for Elisha. "My son, give me your heart."
ISBN 1-56043-166-0

➤ YOU HAVE NOT MANY FATHERS STUDY GUIDE
ISBN 0-7684-2036-9

➤ THE HOUSE THAT GOD BUILT

Beyond whatever man can desire is a God-given pattern for the life of the Church. Here Dr. Hanby unfolds practical applications from the design of the Tabernacle that allow us to become the house God is building today.
ISBN 1-56043-091-5

➤ THE HOUSE THAT GOD BUILT STUDY GUIDE
ISBN 0-7684-2048-2

➤ THE RENEWING OF THE HOLY GHOST

Do you need renewal? Everything in the natural, from birds to blood cells, must either undergo a process of renewal or enter into death. Our spiritual life is no different. With this book, your renewal can begin today!
ISBN 1-56043-031-1

➤ ANOINTING THE UNSANCTIFIED

The anointing is more than a talented performance or an emotional response. In this book, Dr. Hanby details the essential ingredients of directional relationship that allow the Spirit of God to flow down upon the Body of Christ—and from us to the needs of a dying world.
ISBN 1-56043-071-0

➤ PERCEIVING THE WHEEL OF GOD

On the potter's wheel, a lump of clay yields to a necessary process of careful pressure and constant twisting. Similarly, the form of true faith is shaped by a trusting response to God in a suffering situation. This book offers essential understanding for victory through the struggles of life.
ISBN 1-56043-109-1

Available at your local Christian bookstore.

For more information and sample chapters, visit www.destinyimage.com